SCAPIN, TRICKSTER

Molière

translated & adapted by

Matt DiCintio

BROADWAY PLAY PUBLISHING INC
New York
www.broadwayplaypub.com
info@broadwayplaypub.com

SCAPINO THE TRICKSTER
© Copyright 2022 Matt DiCintio

All rights reserved. This work is fully protected under the copyright laws of the United States of America. No part of this publication may be photocopied, reproduced, stored in a retrieval system, or transmitted, in any form or by any means, electronic, mechanical, recording, or otherwise, without the prior permission of the publisher. Additional copies of this play are available from the publisher.

Written permission is required for live performance of any sort. This includes readings, cuttings, scenes, and excerpts. For amateur and stock performances, please contact Broadway Play Publishing Inc. For all other rights please contact the author c/o B P P I.

Cover art by Johann Stegmeir

First edition: September 2022
I S B N: 978-0-88145-932-6

Book design: Marie Donovan
Page make-up: Adobe InDesign
Typeface: Palatino

SCAPINO THE TRICKSTER was commissioned by the University of Richmond Department of Theatre & Dance. It was produced there in September 2021. The cast and creative contributors were:

ARGANTE	Liam Keenan
GERONTE	Gabriel Matthews
OCTAVIUS	Adita Narayanan
LEANDER	Quan Chau
ZERBINETTA	Joan Zhao
HYACINTH	Sanjna Kaul
SCAPINO	Benjamin Cudmore
SYLVESTRO	Doro Azizi
NERINA	Allison Martin
ZANNI	Pranay Bhootra
ZANNI	Cameron Peterson
Director	Walter Schoen
Costumes design	Johann Stegmeir
Scenery	Vicki Davis
Sound & lighting design	Robby Williams
Stage Manager	Paige Willis

CHARACTERS & SETTING

ARGANTE, *father of* OCTAVIUS *and* ZERBINETTA
GÉRONTE, *father of* LEANDER *and* HYACINTH
OCTAVIUS, *son of* ARGANTE, HYACINTH*'s love*
LEANDER, *son of* GÉRONTE, ZERBINETT*a's love*
ZERBINETTA, *long-lost daughter of* ARGANTE, LEANDER*'s love*
HYACINTH, *daughter of* GÉRONTE, OCTAVIUS*' love*
SCAPINO, LEANDER*'s servant, a liar*
SILVESTRO, OCTAVIUS*' servant*
NERINA, HYACINTH*'s nurse*

Naples. A town square with a fountain. Way back when.

for Walter Schoen

Scene One

(OCTAVIUS *and* SILVESTRO, *who is doubled over, panting, out of breath. Throughout,* SILVESTRO *attempts to reach the fountain to drink.* OCTAVIUS *keeps blocking him unwittingly.*)

OCTAVIUS: What terrible news for a heart full of love!

SILVESTRO: Yes, yes, terrible. Very. Terrible.

OCTAVIUS: I'm doomed!

SILVESTRO: Ran. All the way. From the port.

OCTAVIUS: My father arrived just this morning?

SILVESTRO: Just this morning.

OCTAVIUS: And he's determined to see me married.

SILVESTRO: Yes.

OCTAVIUS: To Signore Géronte's daughter?

SILVESTRO: Signore. Géronte.

OCTAVIUS: And the girl was brought all the way from Pino sulla Sponda del Lago Maggiore.

SILVESTRO: Pino sulla Sponda del Lago— *(He takes a break to breathe.)* —Maggiore.

OCTAVIUS: And you've heard this news from my uncle?

SILVESTRO: From your uncle.

OCTAVIUS: To whom my father sent word by letter?

(SILVESTRO *makes a gesture indicating writing.*)

OCTAVIUS: And my uncle knows all our plans?

(SILVESTRO *makes a gesture indicating everything.*)

OCTAVIUS: Well talk!

(SILVESTRO *finally drinks.*)

SILVESTRO: That's all the details, that's all I know.

OCTAVIUS: When my father learns what I've been up to, a storm of spontaneous censure will rain down on me.

SILVESTRO: I'm going to pay for your escapades under a flurry of baton blows.

OCTAVIUS: Sweet Lord! How ever will I find my way out of this?

(SCAPINO *appears.*)

SCAPINO: I hear words of pain, and I arrive. Are you troubled? What's wrong? Who died?

OCTAVIUS: Oh, Scapino, I'm the unluckiest of all men. If you could find some invention that would fly me away from pain, I would be indebted to you all my life.

SCAPINO: I have been blessed from above with a sparkling genius for ingenious escapades to which only the most illiterate vulgarians refer as lies. I find very little to be impossible when I want to get my little fingers in there. Alas, I've been forced to retire since the law and I took a tiny tussle, and she was very rough with me.

OCTAVIUS: Please, Scapino, if only you knew how two months ago Signore Géronte and my father embarked together on a certain journey that involved both their business interests.

SCAPINO: This I know.

OCTAVIUS: And Leander and I were both left by our fathers, me under the supervision of Silvestro, Leander under yours.

SCAPINO: This I know.

OCTAVIUS: Sometime later, Leander met a young woman with whom he fell in love.

SCAPINO: This I know.

OCTAVIUS: As we're great friends, he introduced me to his paramour. I thought she was lovely enough, but not as lovely as he thought I should think her. He talked about her and only her all day every day, exaggerating all day every day how beautiful she was. He chastised me for not being more affected by the fires of his affection.

SCAPINO: And?

OCTAVIUS: And one day, as I was accompanying him to the home of the object of his intentions, we heard, in a little house, a block away, a few cries mixed with more than a few tears. A sighing woman said we could see a sight so sad we'd be moved to our own tears.

SCAPINO: And?

OCTAVIUS: And curiosity ushered us to the hovel, where we saw an old dying woman, a servant in prayer, and a young girl in tears—the most beautiful woman ever known to man.

SCAPINO: Ah…

OCTAVIUS: She was dressed only in a dirty shift and a muslin nightshirt. Her hair was like a nun's, pulled high over her head, with sorrowful strands streaming over her shoulders. Still, she sparkled with a thousand virtues.

SCAPINO: Ah.

OCTAVIUS: She wept with such poise!

SCAPINO: And so you love her.

OCTAVIUS: Oh, Scapino. Such a shallow word for how deeply I feel. I tried to ease her suffering. Later I asked Leander what he thought of her; he had the nerve to say he found her "quite pretty." I didn't care for his tone.

(SILVESTRO, *impatient, stopping* OCTAVIUS)

SILVESTRO: His heart was aflame, he didn't know how to live if he couldn't comfort the grounded goddess, his frequent visits were rejected by the servant-turned-governess. Thus: a man in despair. He begs, he pleads, he bargains, he beseeches— *(He blows a raspberry: bupkis.)* The girl, though dirt poor and dirty, comes from a good family, can't come within a block—love is complicated with complications—he reflects, he wrestles, he reasons, he weighs, he resolves—they've been married for three days.

SCAPINO: I see.

SILVESTRO: The sudden return of his father, the uncle's discovery of the secret marriage, the impending marriage to the girl from Pino sulla Sponda del Lago Maggiore, despair despair et cetera.

SCAPINO: And here you are, a grown man who can't turn up anything in your noodle, no way pave a path with a noble lie, no pleasant little ploy to get what you want? *(He spits.)* I wish someone would give me a couple twilighters to hoodwink.

SILVESTRO: I confess: Heaven hasn't given me your gift for weaseling.

OCTAVIUS: Ah, my dear Hyacinth!

(HYACINTH *enters.*)

HYACINTH: Oh, Octavius! Is it true? Has your father returned. He wants you to marry?

OCTAVIUS: Yes, my lovely Hyacinth. The news is a massacre. —You're crying! Why the tears? Do you doubt the quantity of my love for you?

HYACINTH: I know you love me, Octavius, but I don't know that you'll always love me.

OCTAVIUS: How can I live without loving you?

HYACINTH: I've heard men don't love as long as women do. I've heard the passions men feel are like fires that burn out as easily as they kindle.

OCTAVIUS: My dear Hyacinth, my heart is not made like other men's. I'll love you to the grave.

HYACINTH: Yours or mine? Your father wants you to marry someone else. I think I'll die.

OCTAVIUS: I'd leave the country before I'd leave you. Please, my dear Hyacinth, your tears are stabbing at my heart. Don't cry.

HYACINTH: *(Suddenly no longer crying)* Alright.

SCAPINO: *(Aside)* She's no dummy.

OCTAVIUS: *(Indicating* SCAPINO*)* This man will be our savior.

SCAPINO: I have told the world I'll no longer meddle with the world, but if you both beseech, perhaps—

OCTAVIUS & HYACINTH: We beseech!

SCAPINO: I suppose one must allow oneself to be persuaded for the sake of some humanity.

OCTAVIUS: Thank you, Scapino—!

(SCAPINO *makes a noise to silence him and turns his attention to* HYACINTH.)

SCAPINO: You go, and be at ease.

(HYACINTH *leaves.* SCAPINO *turns to* OCTAVIUS.)

SCAPINO: And you, prepare to hold firm against your father's onslaught.

OCTAVIUS: Yes, though I'm quite shy, myself, you see.

SCAPINO: You must stand firm from the very first volley. Show some backbone. Stiffen up. Here, let's practice. Stern face, head up, eyes fixed.

OCTAVIUS: Like this?

(SCAPINO *hits* OCTAVIUS *to adjust his posture.*)

SCAPINO: Better. Now imagine I'm your father, I'm coming, now— Grit and gumption! "How dare you, you good-for-nothing brat, hell spawn, vile ingrate, thankless sunuva father who gave you his life— how dare you show your snotty face after reveling in perversion in my absence?" (*He hits him again.*) Better. —"How dare you marry without your father's consent? I knew I should have beaten you more as a child. Answer me, you reprobate!"

(OCTAVIUS *stands there.*)

OCTAVIUS: The resemblance is uncanny…

SCAPINO: All the more reason to speak up!

(OCTAVIUS *stands there, then:*)

OCTAVIUS: I'm going to go find some courage.

SCAPINO: Your father's coming.

OCTAVIUS: *(Fleeing)* Precious Lord, I'm done for!

SCAPINO: There goes a pretty picture.

SILVESTRO: Here comes Argante.

SCAPINO: Just follow my lead.

(ARGANTE *enters but thinks he's alone.*)

ARGANTE: Has anyone ever heard of such a damned thing?

SCAPINO: *(To* SILVESTRO*)* He already knows.

ARGANTE: I'll throw that runt of a son in a hole! And I'll beat the breath out of that numbskull Silvestro.

SILVESTRO: *(To* SCAPINO*)* It's nice to be remembered.

ARGANTE: *(Noticing* SILVESTRO*)* Oh! Here you are, sage family saint, eagled-eyed keeper of children.

SCAPINO: Signore, you're back! I can't contain myself.

(ARGANTE *moves on* SILVESTRO.)

ARGANTE: You followed my orders to a perfect T, haven't you? My son behaved like a real whiz under your supervision.

SCAPINO: *(Stepping between them)* I did hear about a certain some small thing or other.

ARGANTE: A son marrying without his father's permission is some small thing?!

SCAPINO: I wouldn't think so much a fuss would be made over it.

ARGANTE: I do think so much a fuss would be made over it, and I'll make so much a fuss over it so long as I feel like making the fuss!

SCAPINO: It isn't the worst thing in the world. I could think of much worse—nothing I've ever done, of course not, no.

ARGANTE: What could be worse?

SCAPINO: I would think about it in context. A certain Leander in whose employ I may be may have committed a far darker sin than your son's wee indulgence. A similar sin, Signore, but a sin far *deeper*...

ARGANTE: He always was an idiot.

SILVESTRO: Which one?

ARGANTE: And I don't give a fruit about other people's idiots.

SILVESTRO: Oh, the other one.

SCAPINO: I break my loyalty pledge to him for your sake, Signore, and to show I also have a certain devotion to your son.

ARGANTE: Is that so…?

SCAPINO: That is so and that's the context: Leander cursed his father all the way to the altar, but not Octavius, Signore, not your pride and joy—I'm on your side here—I'd have a little tête-à-tête with your son. I'd scold him mildly for demonstrating insufficient respect instead of extolling my utmost virtues as a father. That's the best of the best options. After all, it was a certain small thing is all.

ARGANTE: What in hell are you talking about? I'm gone two months and Octavius makes a beeline for the first floozy he can find in the alley.

SCAPINO: How could he be as wise as you? Young people are young. Weren't you young once? Indulge a peccadillo here and there? I heard you were on all the ladies' lips.

ARGANTE: I was a gentleman! I never did anything near what my son did.

SCAPINO: He saw someone who saw him—he gets that from you, all the women and all—he thought she was lovely. He visited her, he spoke to her softly, he sighed passionately—but very politely. She responded. —SURPRISE! her parents walk in, raise their fists, drag them to church. What should he have done? Fought them? Better married than dead.

SILVESTRO: *(Aside)* Is that true?

ARGANTE: I didn't know that's how it came about.

SCAPINO: *(Pointing* SILVESTRO*)* Ask him, he'll tell you.

ARGANTE: They were married by force?

SILVESTRO: Oh, yes, Signore.

ARGANTE: Then we must find a judge immediately.

SCAPINO: He doesn't want that.

ARGANTE: It'll be easy to end the marriage.

SCAPINO: End the marriage!

ARGANTE: Yes.

SCAPINO: You can't end the marriage.

ARGANTE: I can't end the marriage?!

SCAPINO: No.

ARGANTE: I'm the father, and my son was threatened.

SCAPINO: He won't consent.

ARGANTE: He won't consent?

SCAPINO: No.

ARGANTE: My son.

SCAPINO: Your son. Why not just have him stand in the street with a sign that says, "My belly is yellow; do with me as you please?" No, no, for his honor and yours, you must say he married her of his own free will.

ARGANTE: And for my honor and his, he should say the opposite.

SCAPINO: No. I'm sure he won't.

ARGANTE: I'll make him.

SCAPINO: He won't, I tell you.

ARGANTE: He will, or I'll disown him.

SCAPINO: You?

ARGANTE: Yes, me.

SCAPINO: Fine.

ARGANTE: What, fine?

SCAPINO: You won't disown him.

ARGANTE: I won't disown him?

SCAPINO: No.

ARGANTE: Who will stop me?

SCAPINO: You will.

ARGANTE: Me?

SCAPINO: You won't have the heart.

ARGANTE: I'll have it.

SCAPINO: A father's duty will do its duty.

ARGANTE: It'll do nothing.

SCAPINO: Nonsense.

ARGANTE: Not nonsense!

SCAPINO: You're too good by nature.

ARGANTE: I'm mean when I want to be. —You're giving me an ulcer. *(He turns to* SILVESTRO.*)* Go on, Lazy, go get that fool. I must now share my disgrace with Signore Géronte. *(Leaving. To himself)* Why do I only have a son? Where is the daughter Heaven took from me…?

SILVESTRO: Octavius and Leander will be in your debt!

SCAPINO: My debt?

SILVESTRO: Most surely.

SCAPINO: *(Light bulb)* My debts! That tiny tussle with the law? I stole some money and the nickel-and-dimers have the audacity to want it back. I think this can work out for everyone… First, you must be incognito. We'll need to disguise your voice.

(SCAPINO *grabs his crotch.*)

(SILVESTRO *yelps.*)

SILVESTRO: *(Falsetto)* Okay.

SCAPINO: *(Hitting him somewhere else)* That won't work.

SILVESTRO: *(Deep)* Better?

SCAPINO: This is my greatest plan yet! *(He struts off.)*

(SILVESTRO *follows* SCAPINO *very delicately.*)

Scene Two

(ARGANTE *and* GÉRONTE *have entered.*)

GÉRONTE: Yes, yes, they should be here by now. My man in Pino sulla Sponda del Lago Maggiore saw them board the ship. It isn't my daughter's best timing, but your son's little escapade is no boon either.

ARGANTE: Don't give yourself the agita, I'll fix it.

GÉRONTE: The education of children oughtn't be a thing to be "fixed."

ARGANTE: Is that so?

GÉRONTE: Children's bad behavior is behavior learned from bad parents.

ARGANTE: And your son's behavior has been straight-laced and stand-up?

GÉRONTE: What have you heard about my son?

ARGANTE: Your man Scapino was only too happy to share all the details, and I'm too happy to share them with my attorney.

(ARGANTE *goes, as* LEANDER *enters, running, out of breath. He goes to embrace* GÉRONTE.)

LEANDER: Father! You're back!

(GÉRONTE *rebuffs* LEANDER.)

GÉRONTE: Easy, boy.

LEANDER: *(Attempting to embrace him again)* Father! But I'm overjoyed!

GÉRONTE: *(Rebuffing)* We need to have a conversation or two.

LEANDER: *(Attempts to embrace him again)* We do?

GÉRONTE: *(Rebuffing)* Back off, you whelp.

(LEANDER *steps back then attempts to embrace* GÉRONTE *again.*)

GÉRONTE: *(Moving away)* What have you done since I've been away?

LEANDER: Nothing to displease you.

GÉRONTE: You're sure?

LEANDER: I'm sure I'm innocent.

GÉRONTE: Scapino shared some news.

LEANDER: Scapino?!

GÉRONTE: We will not air this in public. I'll see you at home, and then I'll decide if I'll disown you.

(LEANDER *goes to embrace him again; he ends up on the ground as* GÉRONTE *exits.*)

(SCAPINO *and* OCTAVIUS *have entered.*)

OCTAVIUS: My dear friend, I thank the High Heavens for you.

(*From the ground,* LEANDER *tries to attack* SCAPINO.)

LEANDER: Judas will be punished!

SCAPINO: *(Fleeing and bowing)* Your servant, as ever.

LEANDER: *(Drawing his sword)* You can't keep your mouth shut?!

SCAPINO: *(Dropping to his knees)* Signore!

(OCTAVIUS *intervenes.*)

LEANDER: Let me at him!

OCTAVIUS: *(Holding him)* Please!

LEANDER: *(Fighting* OCTAVIUS*)* I just want to drown him in this fountain.

SCAPINO: What did I do?

LEANDER: *(Drawing his sword)* You did what you did!

OCTAVIUS: *(Holding* LEANDER*)* Easy!

LEANDER: I want him to own up to his bunco betrayal. I know what you did, and I want a confession from your filthy mouth, or I'll remove your guts.

SCAPINO: Something I said?

*(*LEANDER *moves to slice* SCAPINO.*)*

SCAPINO: Signore! I confess, I confess! I confess my friends and I drank that bottle of Spanish wine you've been saving. I confess I was the one who refilled the bottle with piss and vinegar so you wouldn't know.

LEANDER: You drank my wine?! *(He thinks for a beat, then rushes to the fountain and washes out his mouth.)*

SCAPINO: I ask for your forgiveness.

LEANDER: That's good to know, I suppose. —But that's not what I'm talking about!

SCAPINO: It's not?

LEANDER: No!

SCAPINO: I don't remember anything else.

LEANDER: *(Going for him)* Oh, you don't, do you?

OCTAVIUS: *(Intervening)* Easy…

SCAPINO: I'm sorry, I'm sorry. Three weeks ago that night you sent me out to give that watch to that woman you're fixed on, and I came back all covered in filth, my face all bloody because thieves had beaten me and left me in the mud and stole the watch? I kept the watch.

LEANDER: You stole my watch?

SCAPINO: I needed more time.

*(*LEANDER *looks at* SCAPINO.*)*

(Then he moves on him.)

LEANDER: —That's not the treason I'm talking about!

SCAPINO: It's not?

LEANDER: *(Nearing stabbing him)* Talk fast!

OCTAVIUS: *(Intervening)* Please!

SCAPINO: Except for that time, you remember that time that night that werewolf snuck up on you and nearly broke your neck and beat you to within a smidge of your life?

LEANDER: And?!

SCAPINO: I don't believe in werewolves.

(LEANDER *stabs at* SCAPINO.)

SCAPINO: I was doing you a favor! I wanted you to be afraid of the dark so you'd stop sneaking out at night.

LEANDER: What did you tell my father?

SCAPINO: Your father?

LEANDER: Yes!

SCAPINO: Haven't seen him. He'll tell you himself.

(SILVESTRO *rushes in.*)

SILVESTRO: *(Falsetto)* Signore! *(Clears his throat, normal voice)* I have terrible news. Her family—Zerbinetta's family is taking her away. She told me to tell you if you don't come up with the money they demanded in two hours, you'll lose her forever.

LEANDER: Two hours?

SILVESTRO: Two hours.

(Beat)

(LEANDER *looks toward* SCAPINO.)

LEANDER: My friend! Help me!

SCAPINO: "My friend"?

LEANDER: I forgive you for everything you just told me and everything you haven't.

SCAPINO: No no, thank you, you may now stab me to death.

LEANDER: No, save my love—save my life!

SCAPINO: Go ahead, remove my guts.

LEANDER: I need your guts!

OCTAVIUS: For Heaven's sake, Scapino.

LEANDER: Forgive my behavior, please!

SCAPINO: I am offended.

OCTAVIUS: Scapino…

LEANDER: You'd leave me in my hour of torment!

SCAPINO: You tried to remove my bowels.

LEANDER: *(Groveling)* With all my heart, forgive me! I'm on my knees, I'm in the dirt, don't leave me!

OCTAVIUS: Get him up.

SCAPINO: *(Helping him up)* Don't jump to conclusions next time.

LEANDER: So you'll help me?

SCAPINO: I need some time to think.

LEANDER: Time is running out!

(SCAPINO checks his watch.)

SCAPINO: Don't strain yourself. How much do you need?

LEANDER: Five thousand florin.

SCAPINO: What about you?

OCTAVIUS: Two thousand.

SCAPINO: I think I'll get it from your fathers. *(To* OCTAVIUS*)* You'll be taken care of shortly. *(To*

LEANDER) And your father, that miserable miser, he'll believe anything I want him to believe. There's Signore Argante now. Off you both go. *(To* SILVESTRO*)* You come back in a minute—just as we discussed.

(OCTAVIUS *and* LEANDER *go.*)

(ARGANTE *enters.*)

ARGANTE: Insubordinate mutt…!

SCAPINO: Signore, your servant.

ARGANTE: Hello, Scapino.

SCAPINO: You mentioned your son…?

ARGANTE: I'm in mourning.

SCAPINO: Signore, our lives are full of challenges. We must steel ourselves! You're familiar with the old saying.

ARGANTE: What old saying?

SCAPINO: When a father is gone, he must be even more present. Houses can burn, money can fly, wives can flee, sons can be slaughtered, daughters can rebel. Caution equals good fortune. Just my philosophy. Now, me, I never go home without assuming my employers are in a rage—yelling, beating, kicks in the ass, switches, belt buckles—and when nothing happens, good fortune for all.

ARGANTE: But I cannot suffer this marriage. I've just talked to my attorney.

SCAPINO: But the public record, Signore.

ARGANTE: What else can I do?

SCAPINO: Your rage has lit the flame of my compassion. I find fathers seething at their sons very moving.

ARGANTE: I thank you.

SCAPINO: I've located the woman's brother. You know the type, all mouth and sword, would just as soon knife a friend as chug a glass of wine. I told him about the marriage, your rights as a father, your appeal to the rule of law, your money, your friends, your penchant for out-of-proportion violence. He was sympathetic. He'll end the marriage for a tidy sum.

ARGANTE: How much?

SCAPINO: It's much too much.

ARGANTE: How much?

SCAPINO: Five thousand florin. Six thousand.

ARGANTE: Is he deranged?

SCAPINO: I told him you were no fool—he disagreed—he said he was joining the army and needed at least a thousand for a horse.

ARGANTE: A thousand for a horse, done.

SCAPINO: Plus the harness and a pistol.

ARGANTE: That's two thousand, maybe.

SCAPINO: And a horse for his valet.

ARGANTE: Let him walk!

SCAPINO: Signore…

ARGANTE: He gets nothing.

SCAPINO: You want his valet to walk?

ARGANTE: He can tiptoe for all I care.

SCAPINO: Signore, think of the publicity a trial—

ARGANTE: Fine.

SCAPINO: He also wants a mule.

ARGANTE: His ass can go to hell! I'll see them in court!

SCAPINO: Signore…

ARGANTE: Nothing.

SCAPINO: A little ass.

ARGANTE: Not a little ass and not a big ass!

SCAPINO: Signore…

ARGANTE: I'd rather sue.

SCAPINO: Are you familiar with the justice system? The courts are a maze.

(ARGANTE *looks at* SCAPINO.)

SCAPINO: I've heard. *(Beat)* The *forum non conveniens*, the *in personam* which could lead to *in pari delicto*. Not to mention the secretaries, lawyers, clerks, judges, servants—all grifters. None of those animals would miss the opportunity to manhandle Lady Justice. One wink from a bailiff, you're guilty as sin. Your attorney will sell you like a side of beef. Facts don't matter, and the other attorney will make sure that's true. And if, *if,* by some impossible luck, you make it through the gauntlet, the judge will rule you're at fault and everyone who is at fault is not. And, if, *if,* you're not burned by that whole hell, the press will say you are.

ARGANTE: How much is that mule?

SCAPINO: Signore. For the mule, the horse, the valet's horse, the harness, and the pistol: five thousand florin. Six thousand.

ARGANTE: Six thousand?

SCAPINO: Yes.

ARGANTE: I'll sue!

SCAPINO: You need money to sue. Court costs are expensive.

(ARGANTE *looks at* SCAPINO.)

SCAPINO: I hear. You need filing fees, court fees, deposition fees, discovery fees, transcription fees, days and days and nights of attorneys' fees. The clerk fees, the bailiff fees, the secretary's fees. Those alone will easily run you five thousand florin. Six thousand.

ARGANTE: I will not give that man five or six thousand florin!

(SILVESTRO *enters in disguise.*)

SILVESTRO: Where is this Signore Argante?

SCAPINO: Why?

SILVESTRO: I hear he wants to sue me over my sister's marriage.

SCAPINO: I don't know about that, but he's not going to pay you.

SILVESTRO: I'll murder him! I'll scalp him! I'll snap his neck!

(ARGANTE *hides.*)

SCAPINO: Signore, he's a brave man. He won't be afraid of you.

SILVESTRO: I want to see his blood! *(He draws his sword.)* Who's that?

SCAPINO: No one, it's no one.

SILVESTRO: One of his friends?

SCAPINO: It's his mortal enemy, Signore.

SILVESTRO: His mortal enemy?

SCAPINO: Yes.

SILVESTRO: Excellent! You're the mortal enemy of that imbecile Argante?

SCAPINO: He is, he is.

SILVESTRO: *(Shaking* ARGANTE's *hand roughly)* I give you my word and upon my honor, upon my sword and every oath I can make: before the day is done, that vermin Argante will see justice.

SCAPINO: Violence is frowned upon in these parts.

SILVESTRO: I've got nothing to lose!

SCAPINO: He has guards, I'm sure. Plus family, friends, servants. They'll save him.

SILVESTRO: I'll take them all! *(He waves his sword as though he's fighting multiple people.)* Head! Heart! Entrails! I hope he's got a dozen men with him! I'll level them all! —Fool! You dare attack me? Death! No mercy! Come at me. Time to meet your maker! —Is that all you've got, you scoundrel? Have a little of this! Have a little of that!

SCAPINO: Signore, please!

SILVESTRO: That's just a preview.

SCAPINO: Look at how many people are dead over a measly five thousand florin. Six thousand.

ARGANTE: *(Trembling)* Scapino…

SCAPINO: Signore?

ARGANTE: I'll pay.

SCAPINO: Inspired choice!

ARGANTE: I have the money at home.

SCAPINO: Please, allow me. I'll spare you the shame of going yourself.

ARGANTE: I'll see this through.

SCAPINO: Don't you trust me?

(ARGANTE *looks at* SCAPINO.)

SCAPINO: Signore, I'm a sinner or I'm a saint. How could I possibly in the world not-once-in-my-life ever deceive you? But if you don't want my help—

ARGANTE: Wait.

SCAPINO: Heaven knows what I'd do with that money in my hot little hands…

ARGANTE: Go, fine, go, but take precautions!

SCAPINO: *("What me, worry?")* Signore, please…

ARGANTE: I'll wait for you at home. *(He exits, wary of* SILVESTRO.*)*

SCAPINO: *(Looking off)* That one's down, now this one to go. *(To* SILVESTRO*)* Fine work, now go.

*(*SILVESTRO *bows and exits as* GÉRONTE *arrives.)*

SCAPINO: …Oh Lord! Whatever shall we do? Poor Géronte!

GÉRONTE: Poor me?

SCAPINO: Signore, your son…

GÉRONTE: Yes, my son…

SCAPINO: Has fallen fast from favor.

GÉRONTE: How's that?

SCAPINO: I found him in such sorrow. I don't know what you said to him, but I had to distract him from his sadness, so I took him to the port for a walk. There, we saw the most marvelous ship, and a very well-mannered mate invited us aboard for lunch. The fruit was fresh, the fish was fine—just a little drier than the Montepulciano—.

GÉRONTE: Montepulciano?

SCAPINO: Montepulciano, si.

GÉRONTE: No orvieto?

SCAPINO: No orvieto.

GÉRONTE: No gavi di gavi?

SCAPINO: No gavi di gavi.

GÉRONTE: No! Six thousand florin!

SCAPINO: Yes, Signore. In two hours.

GÉRONTE: Damned water dog!

SCAPINO: It's up to you, Signore, to save your son!

GÉRONTE: Why did he get on that ship?

SCAPINO: He couldn't have seen this coming.

GÉRONTE: You go tell that sailor I'll have the law after him.

SCAPINO: In the middle of the ocean?

GÉRONTE: Why did he get on that ship?

SCAPINO: Bad luck?

GÉRONTE: It's time, Scapino, to prove your loyalty.

SCAPINO: How so, Signore?

GÉRONTE: Go tell that sailor to send back my son, and you take his place.

SCAPINO: You must think he's a fool to exchange your son for lowly little me.

GÉRONTE: Why did he get on that ship?

SCAPINO: Remember, Signore, we only have two hours.

GÉRONTE: And he wants…?

SCAPINO: Six thousand florin.

GÉRONTE: Six thousand? Has he no scruples?

SCAPINO: How much do scruples cost exactly?

GÉRONTE: Does he know how much six thousand is?

SCAPINO: I think he has an idea.

GÉRONTE: Does he think six thousand comes out of a horse's fart?

SCAPINO: I don't believe he's under that illusion.

GÉRONTE: Why did he get on that ship?

SCAPINO: Signore, hurry, please.

GÉRONTE: Here's the key to my desk.

SCAPINO: Good.

GÉRONTE: Open it.

SCAPINO: Yes.

GÉRONTE: You'll find a large key on the left.

SCAPINO: Yes.

GÉRONTE: That'll open the attic.

SCAPINO: Yes.

GÉRONTE: In a wicker basket in the corner you'll find a pile of old clothing. Go sell them to the homeless until you get to six thousand florin.

SCAPINO: *(Giving back the key)* Signore, we wouldn't get a hundred florin with that scheme. And not even that in the time we have.

GÉRONTE: Why did he get on that ship?

SCAPINO: —Oh, my poor master! My dear friend, bound for servitude! Let Heaven see I've done all I could. Let God see that only your father is now to blame.

GÉRONTE: Scapino, Scapino, I must get this money.

SCAPINO: Time is short, Signore.

GÉRONTE: Yes, yes, five thousand florin.

SCAPINO: Six thousand.

GÉRONTE: Six thousand?

SCAPINO: Yes.

GÉRONTE: Why did he get on that ship?

(SCAPINO *slaps* GÉRONTE.)

GÉRONTE: Scapino, I just remembered I was just given that amount in gold.

(GÉRONTE *gives* SCAPINO *the purse but doesn't release it right away. Tug of war.* SCAPINO *takes the purse.*)

GÉRONTE: Alright. Go buy back my son.

SCAPINO: Yes, Signore.

(SCAPINO *attempts to leave, but* GÉRONTE *tries to get the purse back.*)

GÉRONTE: And you tell that sailor he's a crook.

SCAPINO: Of course.

GÉRONTE: A man without honor!

SCAPINO: Of course.

GÉRONTE: That I have every right not to give him that money.

SCAPINO: Of course.

GÉRONTE: That he'll be wanted dead or alive.

SCAPINO: Of course.

GÉRONTE: That I can't wait to get my hands on him.

SCAPINO: Of course.

(GÉRONTE *has successfully reclaimed the purse and tries to leave.*)

GÉRONTE: Now go save my son!

SCAPINO: Signore!

GÉRONTE: Yes?

SCAPINO: The money?

GÉRONTE: Didn't I give it to you?

SCAPINO: It's in your pocket.

GÉRONTE: Oh, oh, I'm distracted by distress.

SCAPINO: I can see that.

GÉRONTE: *(Leaving)* Why did he get on that ship?

SCAPINO: If he thinks six thousand was hard to swallow, he's about to choke.

(OCTAVIUS *and* LEANDER *enter.*)

OCTAVIUS: Well, Scapino? Success?

LEANDER: Will you save my love?

(SCAPINO *gives* OCTAVIUS *the purse but not before pocketing some of the money.*)

SCAPINO: What I've extracted from your father.

OCTAVIUS: Scapino, you've saved me!

SCAPINO: *(To* LEANDER*)* Sorry, nothing for you.

LEANDER: *(Going to leave)* Then I shall die. I won't live without Zerbinetta.

SCAPINO: Wait, where are you going?

LEANDER: I have nowhere to go.

SCAPINO: I have something else for you.

LEANDER: You've saved my life!

SCAPINO: But only if you allow me a little vengeance for what your father has done to me.

LEANDER: Anything you want.

SCAPINO: You'll swear it?

LEANDER: On the Bible. Now let's go save my love!

Scene Three

(ZERBINETTA, HYACINTH, SCAPINO, *and* SILVESTRO*)*

SILVESTRO: Ladies, your gentlemen's plans are in progress.

HYACINTH: Wonderful! I long for the company.

ZERBINETTA: I am fine with company, as long as friendship is involved.

SCAPINO: But not love?

ZERBINETTA: Love is harder.

SCAPINO: But what he's done for you. —Requires a little…passion.

ZERBINETTA: I rely on goodness. What Leander has done is no assurance of what he will do. And there's a father.

SCAPINO: I believe arrangements will be made.

HYACINTH: Our destinies are twins, and so are our misfortunes, my friend.

ZERBINETTA: At least you know who your family is. They can assure your happiness, grant a hand in marriage even after the fact. There's no one to come to my rescue.

HYACINTH: But your lover's heart is yours, that's all that matters.

ZERBINETTA: What is this sterling plan of yours to drain that buzzard of his money?

SCAPINO: I have a little revenge in mine which will suit me, as well.

SILVESTRO: You're running the risk of a beating.

SCAPINO: It's my rear, not yours.

SILVESTRO: And you may do with that as you please. But mine—

SCAPINO: Have no fear, my friend. Cowards risk nothing. Go now. I'll find you soon.

(ZERBINETTA, HYACINTH, *and* SILVESTRO *go, as* GÉRONTE *enters.*)

GÉRONTE: Well, Scapino, this thing with my son?

SCAPINO: Your son, Signore, is in a safe place. But now you're the one in the danger, the gravest danger. People are looking for you, and they're going to kill you.

GÉRONTE: Me?

SCAPINO: Yes.

GÉRONTE: Who?

SCAPINO: The brother of your son's wife. Your plan to replace his sister with your daughter has him in a rage, and the rage requires him to murder you in order to restore his honor. All his friends are on the hunt, and all his friends are expert swordsmen. Whole platoons are surrounding your home. If you don't go now, you'll have nowhere to hide.

GÉRONTE: Why should I do, Scapino?

SCAPINO: I tremble for you! —Wait. *(He whirls about, goes to the side to see if anyone is there.)*

GÉRONTE: *(Shaking)* Well?

SCAPINO: *(Coming back)* No, no, it's nothing.

GÉRONTE: Scapino! Get me out of this!

SCAPINO: I want to help. I, too, may in danger.

GÉRONTE: You will be well compensated, I assure you. You can have this coat, after I've worn it a little.

SCAPINO: —I know! Get into this sack and—

GÉRONTE: *(Thinking he hears something)* —What's that?

SCAPINO: Nothing, nothing, nothing. Get in the sack and whatever happens, don't move. I'll carry you on my back, through the frontlines, to your house. We can barricade you there.

GÉRONTE: Yes, yes, that's a good idea.

SCAPINO: The best. You'll see. You'll pay.

GÉRONTE: What's that?

SCAPINO: I said, your enemies will pay. Get in, don't move, no matter what happens.

GÉRONTE: You can count on me. *(He gets into the sack.)*

SCAPINO: An assassin! Hurry! *(Exaggerated German accent)* Where can I find this Géronte? I'd like to murder him. *(To* GÉRONTE, *his own voice)* Don't move. *(German) Schiesse!* I'll hunt him down! *(To* GÉRONTE, *his own voice)* Keep quiet. *(German) Dich!* Bag man! *(Own voice)* Signore. *(German)* How much to tell where is this Géronte? *(Own voice)* You're looking for Signore Géronte? *(German) Da, ficker! (Own voice)* And for what business, Signore? *(German)* What business? *(Own voice)* Yes. *(German) Verdammt*, I'm going to beat him to death. *(Own voice)* Oh, Signore, people of his stature simply aren't to be beaten to death. *(German)* Aren't lying scoundrels to be beaten? *(Own voice)* I beg your pardon, he is neither a liar nor a scoundrel. *(German)* You are friends with this Géronte? *(Own voice)* I am. *(German) Schiesse! (He beats the sack several times.)* Have a little of this! *(Own voice)* Ow! Ooh! Signore! Take it easy! *(German)* You can take that to him! *Auf Wiedersehen! (Own voice, writhing as if he's been beaten.)*

(GÉRONTE *pokes his head out of the bag, weary.)*

GÉRONTE: Scapino, Scapino, no more!

SCAPINO: Signore! I'm bruised, broken, in need of a bromide.

GÉRONTE: I was the one who was beaten.

SCAPINO: Signore, I took the blows for you.

GÉRONTE: I felt them! I still feel them.

SCAPINO: No, Signore, you only felt the tip of rod. I made sure of that.

GÉRONTE: Maybe you should stand a little farther away.

(SCAPINO *shoves* GÉRONTE'*s head back into the sack.)*

SCAPINO: Sshh. Someone is coming. *(Exaggerated Russian accent)* Where is that devil from hell Géronte? *(Own voice, to* GÉRONTE*)* Stay down. *(Russian) Privet!* Tell me, please, where is this Géronte? *(Own voice)* I don't know where he could be. *(Russian)* Please, I wish only to flail him a dozen times upon his back and stab him in his chest three or four times only. *(Own voice)* I assure you, Signore, I have no idea where he could be. *(Russian)* What are you hiding in your sack? *(Own voice)* Nothing at all, Signore. *(Russian)* I think I wish to stab your sack. *(Own voice, to* GÉRONTE*)* Steady now… *(Own voice, to* GÉRONTE.*)* Easy, Signore… *(Russian)* Easy, hunh? *(Own voice)* You have no business with my sack. *(Russian)* You'll open it. *(Own voice)* I will not. *(Russian)* Show me, you fool. *(Own voice)* I will not. *(Russian)* You will not? *(Own voice)* No. *(Russian)* You would prefer a trouncing on your head? *(Own)* Ha! *(Russian)* You like to joke, eh? *(He cries out in his own voice as though he's being beaten, all the while beating the sack.)* Ow! Aye! Ooh! Ow! Aye! Ooh! Ow! Aye! Ooh! *(Russian)* That is lesson we learn for telling joke. *Das vadanya. (He pretends to writhe in pain on the ground.)*

GÉRONTE: *(Poking his head out of the sack)* I am dead!

SCAPINO: I am butchered!

GÉRONTE: Why the devil did he beat me?

SCAPINO: *(Shoving his head into the sack)* Sshh. Some soldiers are standing by! *(Exaggerated French)* Come, come. We weell find zees Gérrrrrrrrrrrrrronte! *(Exaggerated Cockney)* Search every corner in the bloody town 'ere, yeh? I fink 'ee must be 'ere, yeh? *(Exaggerated Italian)* Si, si, zee stunad must be 'errrrrrrrrre, si, si. *(Exaggerated French)* Over 'errrrrrrrrrrre! *(Exaggerated Cockney)* Nah, that bloomin' coward is over 'ere, I fink, yeh? *(Exaggerated Spanish)* I sink zat cabrón is zere! *(Own voice, to* GÉRONTE*)* Keep quiet. *(Exaggerated Cockney)* Ay, mates, I fink we found his flunky. *(Exaggerated Italian.)* I sink zat you tail where-uh ees your-uh mastair-uh? *(Own)* Oh, Signore, please don't hurt me! *(Exaggerated Spanish)* Out weet eet, bastardo!

(Exaggerated French) You speak, *oui*? *(Exaggerated Cockney)* Blimy, don't tempt us, yeh? *(Exaggerated Italian)* Madonna! We weel strrrrrrrrrrrike on your-uh testa!

(GÉRONTE *has poked his head out of the sack, unseen by* SCAPINO, *and watches.*)

SCAPINO: *(Exaggerated Cockney)* Blimy, if fiss gormless git ain't gonna tell us what we want uh know, I fink we cock-up the prat. *(Own voice)* I'd rather suffer mortal blows than give up my master! *(Exaggerated Spanish)* Mierda, I seenk we can make-uh that 'appen! *(Own voice)* Do you as must! *(Exaggerated French)* You weesh to 'ave a good beating, *oui*? *(Own voice)* Ow! *(Exaggerated Spanish.)* Bastardo! *(Own voice)* Aye! *(Exaggerated Italian)* Stunad! *(Own voice)* Ooh! *(Exaggerated Cockney, going to beat the sack.)* Bloody fool!

(SCAPINO *sees* GÉRONTE *standing up. He hands* GÉRONTE *the slapstick. He screams.* GÉRONTE *screams.* SCAPINO *runs off.* ZERBINETTA *enters laughing.*)

ZERBINETTA: *(Hands on her knees)* I need air!

GÉRONTE: What do you find so funny?

ZERBINETTA: Oh, Signore!

GÉRONTE: Laughing at my expense!

ZERBINETTA: Your expense?

GÉRONTE: Yes.

ZERBINETTA: What's at your expense?

GÉRONTE: Did you come to laugh in my face?

ZERBINETTA: I'm not laughing in your face. I just heard the funniest story. What a son did to his father.

GÉRONTE: What a son did to his father? For money?

ZERBINETTA: Yes. Would you like to hear it?

GÉRONTE: I would love to hear this.

ZERBINETTA: I'll tell you, it won't be secret for long, that's for sure. Thanks to the heavy hand of destiny, I found myself living with a pack of vagabonds, roaming from town to town, juggling on street corners for meager rations. When we came here, a young man's eye caught me, and I caught his heart. He followed me everywhere, and like most men, he thought that after only exchanging a few words, our fate together would be sealed. He didn't plan ahead: my pride corrected him. He shared his passion with my people, and they were happy enough to dispose of me for a certain sum. But he is a man, and most men have empty pockets. His father, however, does not. His father, however, is a tight-fisted hyena and presumably the worst specimen on earth. Wait. I've forgotten his name… Help me. Who in this town has a reputation for being a hoggish, stingy, pinchfisted tightwad who'd rather watch his bride burn alive than buy a bucket of water? Do you know him?

GÉRONTE: I assure you I do not.

ZERBINETTA: His name… Something —*onte*…Oronte… —No, Géronte! That's it. That's the creature, that's the moneygrubbing tentacle. Anyway, we were planning to leave town today, and my poor lover was still going to lose me because he was still poor, so his servant was going to sucker the skinflint father. I'll never forget his name: Scapino. The man deserves a statue. This was the plan.

(ZERBINETTA *starts laughing so hard throughout the audience should join her.*)

ZERBINETTA: Scapino told the lock-pocketed jackal… that his son was stolen away to sea…and the kidnapper demanded…a six thousand florin ransom… The old hound struggled mightily in his soul…six thousand florin is six thousand daggers…If only he knew

Scapino was pocketing some of it…He practically had to have the money ripped from his guts…He just kept saying… *(She's in hysterics and says the following like it's the greatest punchline ever.)* "Why did he get on that ship…?"

(ZERBINETTA's *laughter finally dies down, and she notices* GÉRONTE *isn't laughing.*)

ZERBINETTA: You don't think it's funny?

GÉRONTE: I think the young man is an unwise, half-witted whelp who needs a whipping. I think the girl is an addled tart who just informed a lock-pocketed jackal that his family is full of fiends who will soon find their way to the gallows! *(He storms off.)*

(SILVESTRO *runs on.*)

SILVESTRO: What are you doing? Don't you know that man is your lover's father?

ZERBINETTA: I think I made a tiny mistake.

SILVESTRO: What mistake?

ZERBINETTA: I told him everything.

SILVESTRO: Everything?

ZERBINETTA: Everything. Oh well, wasn't he going to find out anyway?

(ZERBINETTA *begins to go, as* ARGANTE *enters.*)

ARGANTE: Silvestro!

SILVESTRO: *(To* ZERBINETTA*)* Go home and stay there.

ARGANTE: You! You and Scapino presume you can lie to my face and presume I'll just lie down like an old hound in the street?!

SILVESTRO: Heavens! Signore, if Scapino lied to you, I wash my hands of the scoundrel. I assure you, mine are clean.

ARGANTE: We'll see, you skunk, I am not to be flim-flammed!

(GÉRONTE *enters.*)

GÉRONTE: Signore Argante, I am maimed with disgrace.

ARGANTE: I am maimed!

GÉRONTE: That villain Scapino lied money out of me.

ARGANTE: That villain Scapino lied money out of *me*.

GÉRONTE: And it was apparently insufficient, how he treated me.

ARGANTE: How he treated you?

GÉRONTE: Details are not important. But he'll pay all his accounts in full.

ARGANTE: I want a confession!

GÉRONTE: Final vengeance will be mine!

(SILVESTRO *has been trying to edge his way off stage.*)

(GÉRONTE *now blocks him.*)

GÉRONTE: And that's not all! Misfortune is the mother of misfortune. Long I've wished for my daughter's return, and today I've learned she has departed Pino sulla Sponda del Lago Maggiore.

ARGANTE: Pino sulla Sponda del Lago Maggiore?

GÉRONTE: We fear she's lost at sea.

ARGANTE: But why send her to Pino sulla Sponda del Lago Maggiore?

GÉRONTE: I had family interests to protect in sending her to Pino sulla Sponda del Lago Maggiore. Who's this?

(NERINA *enters.*)

GÉRONTE: Nurse, what is it?

(NERINA *throws herself to her knees.*)

NERINA: Oh, Signore Pandolpho—

GÉRONTE: You will call me Géronte. Never use that name again.

NERINA: Well, that change caused quite a fuss when we tried to find you.

GÉRONTE: Where is my daughter, and her mother?

NERINA: You daughter, Signore, is nearby. But first I must ask your forgiveness in overseeing her nuptials. It was the only choice I had in your absence.

GÉRONTE: My daughter is married?!

NERINA: Yes, Signore.

GÉRONTE: To whom?

NERINA: To a young man named Octavius, son of certain Signore Argante.

ARGANTE & GÉRONTE: Heavens!

GÉRONTE: Take us to her now.

NERINA: She's just inside here.

GÉRONTE: Go, go. Signore Argante, come, come.

(*They go.*)

(SCAPINO *enters.*)

SCAPINO: Silvestro! What's the word?

SILVESTRO: One: the matter with Octavius is settled. Our dear Hyacinth is Signore Géronte's daughter. It seems happenstance and a father's mandate have met hand-in-hand. Two: the old buzzards have promised to murder you, Géronte first.

SCAPINO: Promises never meant much to me.

SILVESTRO: Be careful, Scapino. The sons may want to see you skinned, too.

SCAPINO: Silvestro…I will lie my way back to peace.

SILVESTRO: They're coming—!

(They exit, as GÉRONTE, ARGANTE, NERINA, *and* HYACINTH *enter.)*

GÉRONTE: Come, daughter. Life will be perfect when we find your mother.

ARGANTE: And here is Octavius, in fact.

*(*OCTAVIUS *and* ZERBINETTA *have entered.)*

ARGANTE: Come, my son, let us celebrate this marvelous adventure of your marriage. Heaven—

OCTAVIUS: *(Not seeing* HYACINTH*)* No, father, your proposals will amount to nothing. I have come to confess.

ARGANTE: But you don't even know—

OCTAVIUS: I know all I need to know.

ARGANTE: I'm telling you that Signore Géronte's daughter—

OCTAVIUS: *(Going to* HYACINTH*)* Is good for nothing. I'll die before I leave my dear Hyacinth. She's the one who has my heart, and will for life.

ARGANTE: Alright, she's yours.

HYACINTH: Octavius, this is my father. I've found him. The skies are clear.

GÉRONTE: Come to my home. I'm tired of this square.

HYACINTH: *(Going to* ZERBINETTA*)* Father, promise me you'll welcome my friend, here. You will when you hear all she's done for me.

GÉRONTE: You want in my home your brother's lover and the very same coquette who flouted, insulted, and vituperated me?!

ZERBINETTA: Signore, I offer a hundred apologies. I never would have spoken to you like that if I'd known it was you. Your reputation precedes you.

GÉRONTE: My reputation.

ZERBINETTA: Precedes you. Very far out front.

HYACINTH: Father, my brother's love for her is no crime. She brims with virtue.

GÉRONTE: And I'm to allow my son to marry this vagrant?

(LEANDER *enters.*)

LEANDER: Father, please, yes, I love her, poor orphan that she is. The family I paid just told me she's from this town, and from an honest family. They kidnapped her at age four. They gave me this bracelet to locate her parents.

ARGANTE: The bracelet… My daughter…

ALL: Your daughter?

ARGANTE: It's her. I can see it in her face.

ZERBINETTA: Father…!

(SILVESTRO *enters.*)

SILVESTRO: Signore! The most dreadful occurrence has just occurred!

GÉRONTE: What is it?

SILVESTRO: Poor Scapino…

GÉRONTE: I'll hang him!

SILVESTRO: Oh, Signore, you needn't go to the trouble. In returning home as all good servants do, a stone block fell on his head and split it open. He's on his way to the pearly gates but asked to stop by here first…

(SILVESTRO *helps in* SCAPINO, *his head wrapped in massive bandages.*)

(Everyone gasps.)

SCAPINO: Oh, oh, Signore, don't look, don't look. I couldn't trade this world for the next without offering my sincerest apologies to anyone I may have offended. My dying breath is yours, Signore, to humbly appeal for your forgiveness for anything and every single thing I've done or may have done that you don't know about.

ARGANTE: Oh, Scapino…I forgive you. Die in peace.

SCAPINO: *(To* GÉRONTE*)* It's you, Signore, I have offended most gravely….

GÉRONTE: Say no more, Scapino. I'll forgive you.

SCAPINO: Even for the beating…?

GÉRONTE: A few scrapes…

SCAPINO: That was some beating I gave you…

GÉRONTE: Ssh… We needn't mention it again.

SCAPINO: And it is I who have now been beaten to death…

GÉRONTE: Peace now…

SCAPINO: But I took such pleasure in pummeling you…

GÉRONTE: I've already forgotten.

SCAPINO: It's with a whole heart, Signore, that you forgive me?

GÉRONTE: I'll forgive you for everything.

SCAPINO: Such peace comes over me…

GÉRONTE: Yes, yes, I'll forgive you when you're dead.

SCAPINO: What's that?

GÉRONTE: *(Tenderly)* If you survive, I'll take it all back.

SCAPINO: Oh! The pain…! The agony…!

ARGANTE: Signore Géronte, please. For the sake of our peace, forgive him unconditionally.

GÉRONTE: No conditions…?

SCAPINO: No conditions.

GÉRONTE: No conditions…

ARGANTE: Come, come, we'll break bread together to seal our peace.

GÉRONTE: I have one condition. If you shall live, you shall live to be punished.

SCAPINO: —Oh, I see the light! Glory! I'm ready, My Father!

ARGANTE: *(To* GÉRONTE*)* What do you want?

GÉRONTE: Since this trickster helped our sons connive their way to connubial bliss, I see the only way to mend his breach is for him to suffer the fate. Marry that nurse!

NERINA: Moi?

GÉRONTE: *(Drawing a knife/sword)* In sickness and in health. In life or in death!

SCAPINO: *(Relenting)* Well, if I must impose on that young—

NERINA: I'm game.

ARGANTE: Then it's settled. Peace has returned and brought with it a daughter, two new sons, and whatever that is. *(Meaning* SCAPINO *and* NERINA*)* Now, let us bless these unions.

(The families retire.)

SCAPINO: Leander, my lord—. Octavius, my friend—.

(But they're gone.)

SCAPINO: They're gone…

(And her idea…)

NERINA: They're gone...

SCAPINO: They're gone!

(SCAPINO and NERINA scamper off arm-in-arm, leaving SILVESTRO alone. He walks to the fountain and sits wearily. He lets out a sigh of relief.)

(Finito)

END OF PLAY